BY GONE LOVE

BY GONE LOVE

YESTERDAY'S DREAMS

Beatrice Kincy Watson

authorHOUSE®

AuthorHouse™
1663 Liberty Drive
Bloomington, IN 47403
www.authorhouse.com
Phone: 1-800-839-8640

Published by AuthorHouse   11/17/2012

ISBN: 978-1-4634-4384-9 (sc)
ISBN: 978-1-4634-4385-6 (e)

Library of Congress Control Number: 2011913192

CONTENTS

1. BYE GONE LOVE 1

2. MY ONE AND ONLY 3

3. MY PAST 4

4. SWEET WILD CHILD 5

5. PRISONER OF LOVE 6

6. THE GIRL IN ME DREAMS 7

7. WISHES 9

8. I LOVE YOU 11

9. TEENAGE LOVE 12

10. IF THIS BE LOVE 14

11. A MAN OR A CAT 16

12. FIRST ANGEL 18

13. FORBIDDEN PORTRAIT 20

14. GOOD-BYE 21

15. MIDNIGHT DREAMS 23

16. FIRST LOVE 24

17. F.Y.R. 29

18. A ROSE SO RED 30

19. THE NAUGHTY RAIN 32

20. CHARLIE 33

21. I WISH I WAS 35

22. WATERMELON PATCH GAL 36

23. THE SEA CREATURE 38

24. TRUE LOVE 39

25. TONIGHT 40

26. TO SOME SPECIAL FRIENDS 42

27. THE LOVE OF MY LIFE 44

28. A TATTERED HEART 47

DEDICATION

TO ROBERT

THANKS FOR THE ROSES

ALSO TO THE FIVE OLD FOLKS

WHOM I LOVE SO VERY MUCH

AND TO MY SISTER

MRS. JESSIE LEE LAGRONE

I LOVE YOU ONE, I LOVE YOU ALL

BYE GONE LOVE

I sat upon a stair
You stood smiling down on me
A devil may care gleam
In your dark mischievous eyes
Dimples in your cheeks
Lopsided beautiful
Handsome smile
Neatly cut ebony hair
So slender, tall and stunning
In your soldier's garbs
I looked up into your eyes
Felt the first stirring of love
I wanted your kiss upon my lips
To be caressed with your finger tips
You to hold me close
Lift me up to womanhood
You promised me your love
I made a vow to wait for you
With the sun shining up above
Your lips met mine
In a passionate kiss of love
But once you'd gone
I heard not one word
At least until my foolish heart
Did we both destroy
In dreams I saw
Another in your arms
I saw you smile
And look upon her with love

Heard you whisper sweet
Passionate words of love
Meant only for mine ears
I felt the horror and the shame
A woman scorned, jilted and
Left alone
So I turned to someone new
To soften the pains of losing you
Then you came home to me
Willing my folly to forgive
But my loyalty I did owe
To a child begotten in a
Senseless act, not love
So I set you free and let
You go
To find some one worthy
Of your love
But what you did not know
Was that my heart would
Follow you
Wherever you did go
So where you are tonight
My love I do not know
But here I sit in sad regret
Loneliness and unhappiness
Because after all these years
I miss and love you still

MY ONE AND ONLY

So very long ago
By chance upon a street
Two strangers did meet
Laughing joking
So happy and carefree
As only the young can be

My name, my address
You did request
Writing it down upon
A brown paper bag
Promising so soon to write

Days to weeks, weeks to months
And months to years did turn
Not one word did I hear from you
Your voice I will never forget
Your name I remember still
In dreams your face I see

Maybe you have forgotten me
To you that wonderful day
Maybe just a forgotten memory
But to me it was my one and
Only chance for love

MY PAST

Looking back running fast
Trying to out run my past
No time for too much fun
Must keep on the run
Can't stop for fear you see
I might catch up with me
Looking back over my
Shoulder
The mistakes I've made
The lies I have told
The old dreams and evil
Schemes are getting bolder
They have come out to take
A stroll
So no time for too much fun
Must keep on the run
Can't stop for you see
I might catch up with me
Oh I have changed at last
Oh pray please let it be
Yet memories of my sad
And lonely past
Keep me looking back
And running fast
For the ghosts of my past
Are revived and running fast
With eager feet I must flee
Can't stop for fear you see
I just might catch up with me

SWEET WILD CHILD

Oh that I could understand this child
So sweet, kind, loving, violent, cruel
And wild
Within her tortured being must live a
Hundreds spirits
For there is none so mean, foolish or bold
So understanding keen of mind
Than this poor mixed up troubled soul
Were she a child of March
Old myths would blame on the wind
Her fickle moods and loving heart
Her sincere or disloyal frame of mind
In her heart angels and demons seem to
Be in rage for control of her soul
In constant battle they engage
Keeping her out of control
She would good, sweet, love
And kind
Perhaps cruel, jealous, cold and sad
Perturbed, happy, contented in mind
Depending on who is in control
Of her soul
You love, you pity, you fear
This troubled child so dear
If only I could dissever the demons
From her soul
Pray of her heart the angels take control
And bring peace to her poor tired
Troubled soul

PRISONER OF LOVE

If you must chain me
Let it be with love
If you must bond me
Let it be with a hug
If me you must enslave
Let it be with your kisses

Let my only torture be
Whenever you are away
From me
Secure me with desire
Rule me with passion
Of fire
Hold me with kindness
Keep me with gentleness

Never forget to tell me
My Darling that you love me
With your lips, your eyes
And your heart
And I will be your slave forever
Warm and secure in your love

THE GIRL IN ME DREAMS

Today in the light of the day
She just passed me by
Without a hello or a bye your leave
Not even a twinkle of her eye
Pretending she didn't even know me
When she know she knows me well
She is the girl in me dreams

She is about five feet five
Weight about one twenty five
Long shapely legs and shoe size five
Big brown eyes and dark curly hair
Dimples in her cheeks, ruby red lips
Lovely golden tan complexion
Smile so sweet, such an angel
And she is in love with me

Last night she held me tight
Kissed me in the moonlight
Under the stars shining bright
Whispered sweet words of love
In my ear
Cried when we had to part
Promised that she would always
Love me
And keep me close to her heart

My Mama thinks that I should
Marry and settle down
She would like a grandbaby or two
And even tho it hurts her so
I know that I can not marry
Until I can marry the only girl
In the world for me
Even tho I don't know her name
She is my one and only love
For she is the girl in me dreams

But today in the light of the day
She just passes me by
Without a hello or a bye your leave
Without a twinkle of her eye
Pretending she didn't even know me
When she know she knows me well
She is the girl in me dreams

WISHES

Out of this whole
Wide world
I don't ask for much
My wishes are but few
Darling, I only want you
You to love me
You, my life to share
To always stay near
Whisperings sweet
Endearments in my ear

Out of this whole wide
World
I don't ask for much
My wishes are but few
Darling I only want you
Maybe a little white house
On a hill
Ivy growing around the
Window sill

A baby or two
A little bit of security
A pet or two
A couple of old friends
To visit
Every now and then
A beat up old jalopy
A few neighbors so true

Out of this whole
Wide world
I don't ask for much
My wishes are few
Darling I only want you

To the world my wishes
May seem so small
Hardly anything at all
But they fulfill my
Every dream
They are all I will ever
Want or need
Because Darling
I only want you

I LOVE YOU

I had heard it not
At least for a very long time
Couldn't seem to remember
When such words
Befell these ears of mine

But today mine eyes did see
Scrawled on a tiny envelope
With a cheap little valentine
Proudly stuck inside

A smile on a little girl's face
Her name I did not know
Yet me she seem to recognize
And proudly said this is for you

I thanked her and walked
Back inside
And mentally made a note
That I must find a gift
A name and an address
For this thoughtful child

Even tho the debt
I can never repay
For scrawled on the pretty
Little valentine
Mrs. Watson I love you
Was what she did say

TEENAGE LOVE

I love thee with my eyes
My ears, my finger tips
My arms, my passion and
My breast

The kiss of my lips
My waking thoughts
My peaceful dreams
You hold me captive
With your charms

How long will I love thee
A moment – a second a minute
An hour, a day, a week-
A month a year
No my darling
I will love you forever

Yet I know sometimes
Hearts grow weary
And lovers drift apart
Still it's in my heart
You'll stay

Be we together or apart
For no matter whom I marry
Nor whose child I carry
I will love you forever

But should fate be kind enough
Our love each new day to rekindle
To render us friends when passions
Dies
Let me walk thru life with you

I will treasure your love, your name
Each gentle touch of your hands
Each word that you whisper to me
For I do believe my Darling
I love you eternally

IF THIS BE LOVE

If this be love
I want no part of it
If this be love
I am better off
For lack of it

For love is foolish
Love is blind
It will never let you
Change your mind

Doesn't the silly thing
Know a woman's heart
Is fickle
It's a woman's rights
To change her mind

So when two lovers
Begin to bicker
And one walks off
Leaves the other behind

Why can't this crazy
Thing call love
Bid them strangers in
Each other mind
Why can't we control
This thing call love

Why does it has to
Bring so much pain
Play so many games
Warp so many hearts

Burn and consume so
Many souls
Tear friends and lovers
Apart
Destroy so many young
Ones hopes and dreams

I know that it is real
As the stars above
Oh but the pains,
The pains the pains
That love can bring

So if this be love
I want no part of it
If this be love
I am better off
For lack of it

For love is foolish
Love is blind
It will never let you
Change your mind

A MAN OR A CAT

It has been said no one
Ever gets old
The only thing that gets old
Is clothes
And sometimes we decorate
Or remodel those

But let's face it my dear
Life has became a drag
When the only way that
You can turn a man's head
Is by carrying your money
In a plastic bag

So if when you were young
You were lucky enough to
Meet a man sweet, loving
Kind and true
Into your life no troubles or
Heartaches he did bring
Made you proud to wear his
Name and his ring

So when he is gone
And you are all alone
Let not some sweet young
Handsome thing come a long
Break your heart and waltz off
With all of you and hubby's hard
Earned money

Just remember a man is a man
A cat is a cat
Both can be a pain in the neck
That's a fact
Each can be sweet, loving
Pretending to be oh so true
But if the man ain't right
Forget about him, Honey
And get yourself a cat
Who will love you even
When your money is gone

FIRST ANGEL

You were not really mines
I just wish you were
Even tho I don't believe
I could love you more
Even if you were
You taught me the meaning
Of love
You smiled and captured
My heart

And even tho we are apart
I still remember you
We met when you were
Yet but small and
Mama you chose me to call
You accepted me as your
Paternal grandmother
Because you didn't have
Any other

I remember the games
We used to play
The sweet funny things
You did say
Yes, I remember you
You I will never forget

For no matter how
They phrase it
Real grandson or step
To me you'll always be
My first grandchild
And I hope that you will
Always love me, pray tell
Because Mama will always
Love Yumel

FORBIDDEN PORTRAIT

Nay – nay I beg you please
Me alone you must leave
Have mercy on me
If you please
I cannot, I will not do it
I am so afraid you see
It might reveal the secrets
Within my soul
Hidden so deep
What if by some mystic
Force
You reach within my heart
My soul
Into the center of my thoughts
And scrip me bare
For all the world to see
The person I've hidden
All of these years
Even from me
So paint no portrait
Take no photo, nay
Not even one sketch
Just let me pretend
That I am sane and
Completely whole
Until I am pardoned
By death
Who will let my secrets
Flee from even from me
And my soul

GOOD-BYE

How do you say goodbye
To apart of your ole lonely heart
A part so sweet and dear
So long so near
Can you ever truly do
With friends so few

How can I just let you walk away
When so many things I want to say
Did you not care
When you broke my heart
Destroyed my trust
And tore my dreams apart

For so many dreams
I had for you
Dreams that you carelessly
Tore apart
And walked away with a part
Of my heart
I will love you forever
You I will never forget

So many things I tried to
Instill in you
Be honest, kind and true
A bit generous and loving too
So how and when did I fail
So run on, my dear
You needed so much more
Than I could give

I hope that you will find
The things you need somewhere
Including love, joy, peace and
Happiness
Mine eyes are filled with tears
So lonely and alone am I
Yet I know I must say good-bye

MIDNIGHT DREAMS

Ebony the silent killer of light
Comes creeping across your room
In the middle of the night
Bringing horror and fright
Turning your beautiful dreams
Into nightmares
In the middle of the night

Only to be chased away
By the moon golden's light
Circled with stars so bright
Bringing back beautiful dreams
Of passionate young love
In the still of the night

Love is such a wonderful thing
And can be expressed in so
Many ways
A hug – a kiss – a fleeting smile
A gentle touch-a caressing look
Lovingly from across a room

The kind things someone do
Yet nothing can compare
To hearing someone say
When it's coming truthfully
From the depth of the heart
Those three little words
I love you

FIRST LOVE

Two front teeth missing
A mischieveious smile upon
His face
Freckles and uncombed hair
Dirty breeches and blue plaid
Flannel shirt
Scuffed untied shoes and
Sloppy rolled down socks

Mama saw him first
Climbing over the fence
Into our yard
Boy, what you doing here
Nothing Ma'am
He said stuttering
Almost out of breath

So low as almost to herself
Mama said
Dat boy is up to something
Gonna grow up to be no good
Then I walked out the door
And there he stood

It was the eyes, his eyes
Compelling, spell binding
Such a very pretty blue
They seem to reach out
And sweep me right inside
So what was a girl to do
But giggle and grin
And offer to share her lollipop
Mama said
Gal, don't you know better den dat
Dat boy can't eat nothing here

He is white and you is black
So he just shook his head
And gave it back
The lollipop that was

But ever so often he came
Over to play when
There were no other kids around
Telling me about his girl friends
While my heart broke with every
Word he spoke
I couldn't tell him how much
I love him
Or how much I needed him
How much I wanted to be with him

He grew up to be a handsome lad
The spitting image of his Dad
Now that he was grown-up and
Too old to come over and play
I worshiped him from afar
And cried each time he drove by
With a lovely young lady in his car

But one day when Mama and Daddy
Were away
He came over to visit for awhile
His hand touched mine
I looked up and smiled
And he bent down and kissed me
Right upon my lips
The kiss I had been waiting for
Ever since I was five
And he was six

What might have happen
We will never have the chance to know
Cause Daddy walked in, eyes wide
What is you trying to do, child
Do you wanna git us all hung
Gal, you know better den dat
Git outta here, boy

Wasn't too long before
We moved away
I met a lot of other boys
But the blue eyed boy
I could never forget
I rued the day we ever met

News travels far and wide
Folks said that he turned out to be
A wild, mean and crazy kid
Driving fast, drinking hard and
Cussing loud
Had a few run ins with the law
Almost drove his folks right
Into their graves
But then to his parents delight
He got married and settled down
Even fathered a child or two
At least that what folks said

Well I did the same
Got married to a good black man
But he never did own my heart
Because my heart belonged to a
Blue eyed kid with sandy hair

My heart followed him
Wherever he did go
About him I read
And treasured every word
But life goes on
For together I knew
We didn't belong

Our parents passed on
I read about his in the newspapers
First his Mom and then his Dad
For him I felt so bad
Mines died together in an
Accident

He called to offer me
His sympathy
I thanked him
Looked up and smiled
He started to hang up
Then paused to say

Tis shame that you and I
Were born fifty years too soon
For I am sure that you know
You were my first love
The only girl I ever loved

F.Y.R.

I need you so much
Much more than I can say
I owe you so much
Much more than I can
Ever hope to repay
You have been kind to me
Gentle in your ways
You have taught me so
Many things

You have even tried to
Change my ways
But I am me
That's all I can ever be
So thanks for accepting me
As I am
A moody mixed up soft hearted
Wise cracking dame

Life with you has not been perfect
Yet I am grateful for the years
That I have spent with you
You have my deepest respect
Who knows but if we had met
Before the world had torn my heart
And scarred my soul
Maybe my wild churning emotions
You could have control and taught
Me how to love

A ROSE SO RED

Roses are red
Violets are blue
My every waken moments
Are filled with thoughts of you

I see your face
I hear your voice
You are the object of my fantasy
My dreams are all of you
In dreams you hold me close

Whisper sweet words of love
Into my ear
Promising me that our love will
Never end
Just like the wedding band of gold
You placed upon finger

I worship you from a far
Keeping a breast of everything
That you do my love
My scraps books are filled with
So many clippings and picture
All of and about you

I was with you in everything
Failures, tears, success and
Happiness
I walked through each phase

Of your life with you
I remember not a time
When my heart was not over
Flowing with love for you
But should we ever meet
Speak not one word to me
My love
Just look upon me and smile
Walk away and leave me
With my beautiful dreams
And my wonderful fantasies
For you will always be my
Perfect love
My one chance for happiness
Years to come
When the world has torn
My heart
And scarred my soul
And lovers has torn my
World apart
And broke my heart
I will remember you
I will sit alone and day
Dream again
Recalling my fantasies
About you
Roses are red
Violets are blue
Never shall there
Ever be
A love so true
Or a rose so red
As sweet as you

THE NAUGHTY RAIN

The leaves are brown
And yellow
Upon the trees
But they should be green
Swaying in the breeze
They are turning brown
Not because it's fall
But just because the rain
Has ceased to fall
In every lover's dreams
Of summer
The trees are green
With lovely flowers growing
Around and between
Every season has it rarity
Even some unique variety
Yet when leaves turn brown
And yellow
In summer instead of fall
And come fluttering down to
The ground
The rain ignoring lovers and
Nature's call
With no reason to be found
You wonder if it just grew angry
And cease to fall
Just because young lovers walks
No more in it
Kissing and holding hands

CHARLIE

An old dog without a name
Or a pedigree
Unwanted and unloved
Never knew a bit of kindness
Nor a care
Kicked and shoved around
Not one bit of love
Has he ever found

But to me, he is special you see
For I am so much like he
Since my one true love has gone
I have been all alone
No one has ever loved nor even
Befriended me

No one except the old dog
Who runs out to meet me
Wagging his tail to greet me
With barks of joy
Waiting impatiently for the
Touch of my hand
The sound of my voice
I have got the old dog
And he has got me

To the world we may be
Just a sad, lonely, old woman
An old sad looking mutt
But we are the best of friends
He took away my loneliness
I saved him from homeliness
I love him and he loves me
Charlie and me, we are family

I WISH I WAS

I wish I were
I wish I were
Oh how I wish I knew
Just what I wish I was

I wish I could
I wish I could
Change myself into
Whatever I would like to be

I think that I would like to be
I think that I would like to be
Oh such torture and misery
For I have no inkling of
Just what I would like to be

I wish I were
I wish I were
Oh how I wish I knew
Just what I wish I was

WATERMELON PATCH GAL

She walks in deep thoughts
Alone in the watermelon patch
A smile creases her face
Remembering a silly phrase

A cute little black pickaninny
Grinning over a big red slice of
Watermelon
Gramma saying
Smell a watermelon child
A nasty snake is lurking around
Somewhere

She walks slowly among
The round and oval melons
Thoughts of yesterday's picnics
Fish fries and bar – b-cues on
The Bayou
Smiles on the faces of blacks,
Whites, tan, brown and yellow
As they bite into a slice of ripe
Red watermelon

A long oval melon catches her eye
She clucks it liking the sound
And sits with legs crossed Indian style
Down upon the ground
Knowing that she should hurry home
For there is so much work to be done
But let hubby wait and wonder
Let the children play
Here in the watermelon patch
A little longer she will stay
Reliving the happiness, pains and
The sorrowful times of her life
And a by gone love of yesterday

THE SEA CREATURE

She sat
She watched
She waited

Eyes gazing out upon the sea
Seeing not the pretty sea shells
Scattered along the beach
Nor the sea gulls flying high
Or the great ships sailing by

The sunlight glistening like diamonds
Upon the white foam dancing playfully
Upon the naughty waves
Hearing not the children's laughter
Nor the grown-ups calling to and fro

She sat
She watched
She waited
For a love that could never be
A love that would never return
From the mysterious sea

TRUE LOVE

I want to feel love
True love before I die
Love to possess me
Burn me, consume me
Hurt me and make
I cry
Ring my heart
Tear me apart

Fill my heart with
Abundant joy
A love for which
I would gladly die
For then and only then
Will I feel completely whole
Or willing to let my body
Give up my soul

Or perhaps now that I am
A wee bit older
And maybe a little wiser too
Maybe I will just settle for
A bit of old fashion sweet
Faithful real love

TONIGHT

Where are you tonight
My love
Are you with someone new
Am I still the one you love
Or have you forsaken me too

Perhaps it was never really love
Maybe I was just a fool to think
It was
A gentle touch, a kind word
So easily misunderstood
By someone who had never
Known true love

I rue the day we met
So sad that I should
Remember it yet
Ere then I had my heart
In control
My emotions never stirred
Nor strolled
For I believed that no lover
Would ever be true
At least not to my heart and me

Until you came a long whispering
Words of love
Making promises causing me
To believe in love
Delight in moonlight, find beauty
in stars above
Letting me feel so beautiful
In your arms

Now that you are gone
I am all alone
I know that there is no such thing
As love
At least not for my heart and me
Tis true I do believe that fate has
Agreed no one would ever love
A poor sad, lonely fool like me

TO SOME SPECIAL FRIENDS

The past is a live and so
Vivid tonight
The many gone souls walks
Upon the path of my mind
I close my eyes, my ears
Yet I see faces
I hear voices from the past
They come not to haunt me

Just to let me once again
Capture a few glorious moments
Moments from my yearned for
But elusive past
Come on sugar, hurry up gal

A few too many times
Told unfunny jokes
A hymn song out of tune
Some laughter, tears and fears
Some disappointments, joys
And dreams
Oh, Lord I remember them all

All of the beautiful memories
I hold so dear
Even the things I yearn to forget
The lies, the pains, the regrets
And all of the unhappy moments
Upon these souls I did bring
Oh, God some how please let
They know
That I am sorry, so sorry
For all of the troubles
I brought them

For all of the pains
I may have caused them
I pray that they are free
Captured only for a moment
In my troubled mind
Forever free, free of me
Free of all the emotions
That lived within each tortured
Or troubled soul
Free of this sad, sick world
And living happily with thee
Forevermore
Oh my God in eternity

THE LOVE OF MY LIFE

I sit alone
In my lonely room
Staring upon our
Wedding photo
A handsome groom
In a black tuxedo
A beautiful bride in lace
And satin of white
A picture of you and I
So very long ago

I missed your gentle touch
Hearing you say that
You love me
Walking in the rain
Holding your hand
You are gone now
Angels took you away
I tried to be brave
I didn't want you to see
Me cry

You didn't want to
Leave me
But you were so weak
And tired
You had suffered for
Oh so long
So I kissed you and

Set you free
You smiled, whispered
Good bye
In a fleeting moment
You were gone
And I was all alone

Oh but tonight
You were here
For just a while
I heard your voice
I saw your rugged smile
Felt the touch of your hand
As you handed me a rose
As in the days of old
A lopsided mischief smile
That old gleam in your eyes
Yet your presence I muse deny

For who would believe
That tonight
You were here with me
Your face, your smile
I did see
The world would think
Me insane
If I were to tell them
That I felt
The touch of your hand

Or heard your voice
So gently speak to me
But be that as it may
I know that it is true
Somewhere beyond
The sunset, my love
You wait for me
So soon we will be
Together

But until that day
If only in my dreams
I will see your face
I will hear your voice
I will treasure the roses
You bring to me
Until we are together
My love, forever more
In eternity

A TATTERED HEART

How can I leave you
When I love you so
How can I stay with you
When to others I must go

My heart longs to be with you
Yet it yearns to be with others too
For my heart is a fickle heart
That wishes it could part

Like the families that were once
So close
But now so very far a part
Scattered lke the petals of a rose
Chased around by my lonely heart

With love I leave you
Praying that God will keep you
Until we are all together again
For then and only then
Will my poor ole heart
Be whole again